BUILDING A SUBWAY

BY ANNIE C. HOLDREN

SEQUENCE

AMICUS | AMICUS INK

Sequence is published by Amicus and Amicus Ink
P.O. Box 1329, Mankato, MN 56002
www.amicuspublishing.us

Library of Congress Cataloging-in-Publication Data
Names: Holdren, Annie C. (Annie Cody), author.
Title: Building a subway / by Annie C. Holdren.
Description: Mankato, MN : Amicus and Amicus Ink, [2020] | Series: Sequence amazing structures | Includes bibliographical references and index. | Audience: Grade 4 to 6.
Identifiers: LCCN 2019006255 (print) | LCCN 2019007637 (ebook) | ISBN 9781681518725 (pdf) | ISBN 9781681518329 (library binding : alk. paper) | ISBN 9781681525600 (pbk. : alk. paper)
Subjects: LCSH: Subways--Juvenile literature. | Tunnels--Juvenile literature.
Classification: LCC TF845 (ebook) | LCC TF845 .H58 2020 (print) | DDC 625.4/2--dc23
LC record available at https://lccn.loc.gov/2019006255

Editor: Wendy Dieker
Designer: Ciara Beitlich
Photo Researcher: Shane Freed

Photo Credits: Getty/Sergey Yuzhakov/EyeEm cover; iStock/anouchka 5; iStock/jdwfoto 6; Shutterstock/Dr Morley Read 9; iStock/andresr 10–11; iStock/MoMorad 13; Getty/Stefano Montesi/Corbis 15; AP/Richard Vogel 16–17; Getty/David McNew 19; Getty/Susana Gonzalez/Bloomberg 20–21; iStock/Cylonphoto 23; Alamy/Andreas Teich 24–25; iStock/Kinwun 26–27; iStock/AlxeyPnferov 28

Printed in the United States of America

HC 10 9 8 7 6 5 4 3 2 1
PB 10 9 8 7 6 5 4 3 2 1

TABLE OF CONTENTS

We Need a Subway

The city has a traffic problem. Cars jam the roads. Buses are busy and full. There is no more room for roads. The city's government comes up with a solution. They can build a subway. Subway trains run through tunnels under the city's streets. It will not be an easy project. It will take fifteen years to finish! The city gets started.

LOADING . . . LOADING . . . LOADING . . .

Traffic is a problem in the city. A subway could help people get around faster.

LOADING . . . LOADING . . . LOADING . . .

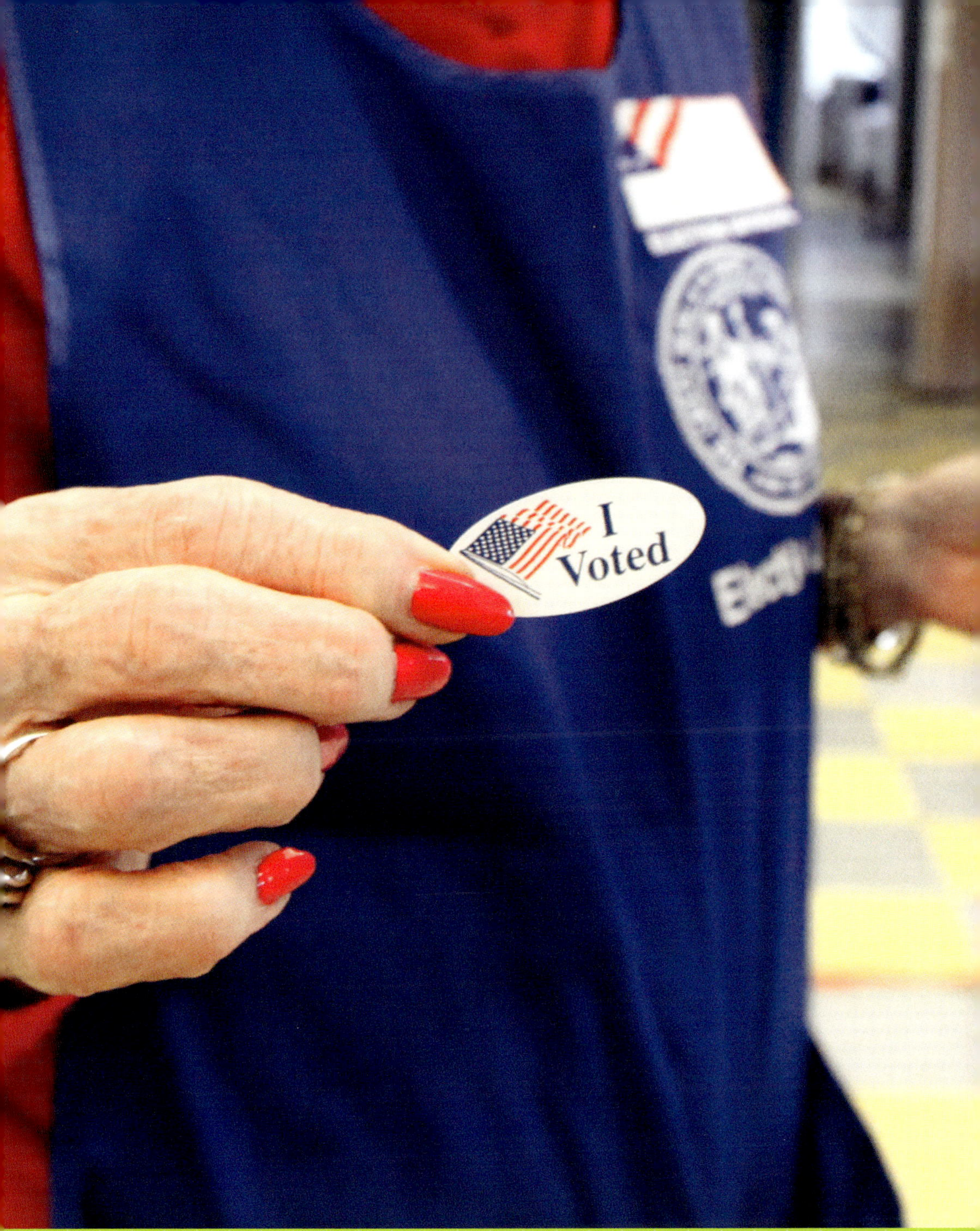

People vote to build a new subway.

YEAR 1

LOADING . . . LOADING . . .

It will cost a lot of money to build a subway. The first step is to find out if the city's people agree to build a subway. The government takes a vote. The people say yes! They also vote for a sales tax. The tax will add a few cents to everything they buy. It will help pay for the subway.

Cities hold elections so people can vote about how taxes will be used.

OADING . . . LOADING . . . LOADING . . .

Time to Plan

Now the city hires **civil engineers**. The engineers start by figuring out where it will be safe to dig. They look for problems like **earthquake faults**. They make sure water does not flow through the soil. Then, they write reports and draw maps. They show where subway tunnels and **stations** should be built. This takes two years to complete.

People vote to build a new subway.

YEAR 1

YEAR 3

Civil engineers report where it will be safe to dig.

ING . . . LOADING . .

Engineers study layers of soil where the subway will go.

LOADING . . . LOADING . . . LOADING . . .

People vote to build a new subway.

Architects and civil engineers give the city a complete plan.

YEAR 1

YEAR 3

YEAR 5

. . . LOADING . . .

Civil engineers report where it will be safe to dig.

Now the civil engineers work with **architects** to plan the subway. The architects draw designs for the train stations. The engineers make sure the designs will work. The subway will have three stations. Two tunnels will be built between each of them. This will let trains travel in different directions.

Architects draw diagrams to show how the tunnels and subway stations will look.

Starting Construction

After six years of planning, finally the digging can begin. The city has hired a company to manage the project. This company is called the **contractor**. The city also has bought two **tunnel-boring machines (TBMs)** for the project. The TBMs will drill through rocks and soil underground. They are as big around as the subway tunnels will be.

People vote to build a new subway.

YEAR 1

Civil engineers report where it will be safe to dig.

YEAR 3

Architects and civil engineers give the city a complete plan.

YEAR 5

The city orders TBMs and hires a contractor.

YEAR 6

LOADING . . .

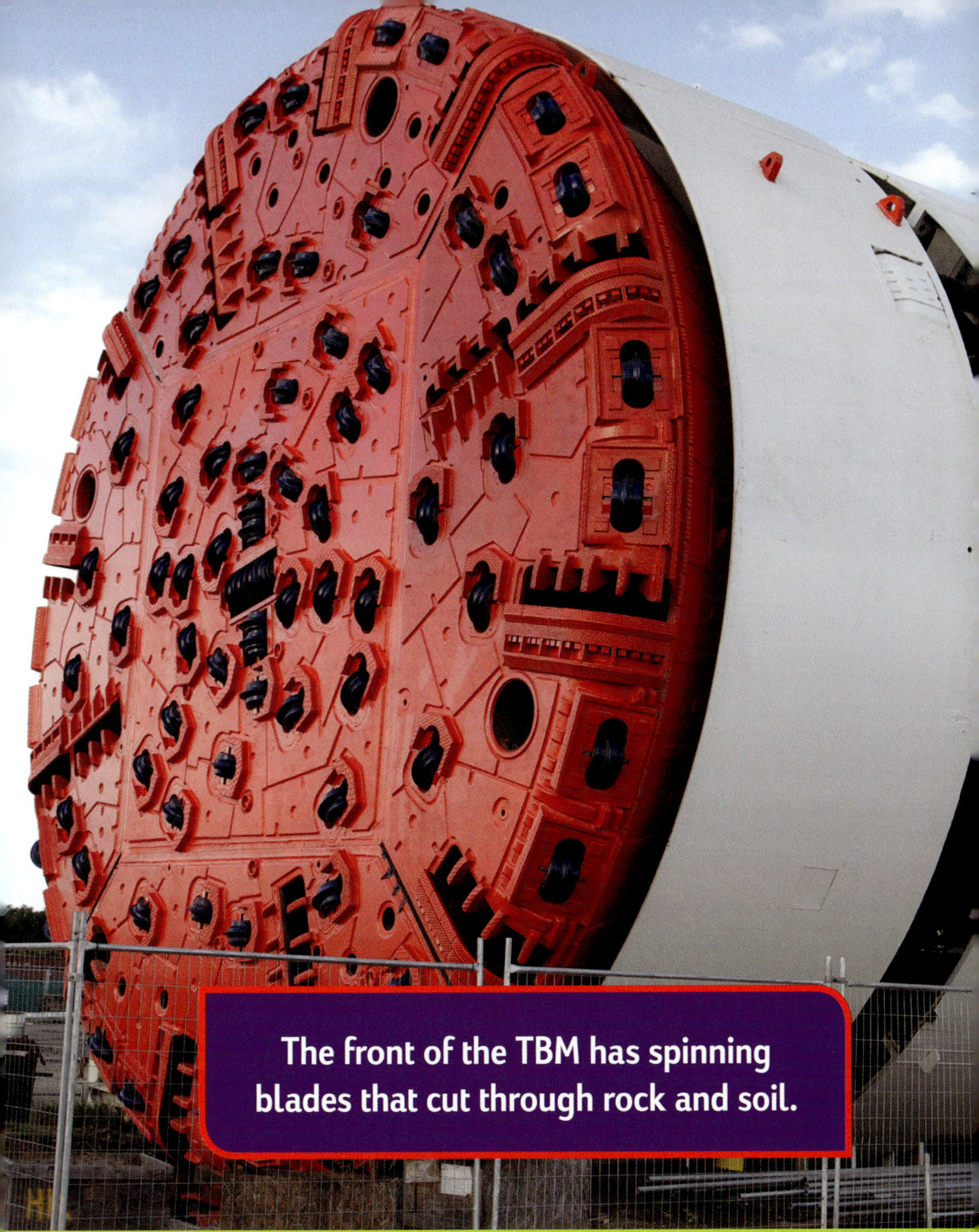

The front of the TBM has spinning blades that cut through rock and soil.

OADING . . . LOADING . . . LOADING . . .

The workers make three huge pits in the ground. The pits will be about one mile apart from each other. They are where the stations will be built. They are also where the TBMs will start drilling tunnels. Workers dig these **launch pits** using machines called **excavators**. The city closes streets where they dig. Cars on the streets must take **detours**.

- YEAR 1: People vote to build a new subway.
- YEAR 3: Civil engineers report where it will be safe to dig.
- YEAR 5: Architects and civil engineers give the city a complete plan.
- YEAR 6: The city orders TBMs and hires a contractor.
- YEAR 7: Construction workers begin digging big pits in the ground.

The area where the tunnel drilling will start is blocked off for safety.

OADING . . . LOADING . . . LOADING . . .

- YEAR 1: People vote to build a new subway.
- YEAR 3: Civil engineers report where it will be safe to dig.
- YEAR 5: Architects and civil engineers give the city a complete plan.
- YEAR 6: The city orders TBMs and hires a contractor.
- YEAR 7: Construction workers begin digging big pits in the ground.
- YEAR 8: **Workers put together the TBM parts.**

When done, each pit is as long as a city block. Construction workers have lined the pits with concrete and steel. Now they use cranes to lower big parts of each TBM into two of the pits. When everything is there, workers put the parts together. It takes a year to get the machines ready.

A worker helps guide a giant TBM part into the launch pit.

OADING . . . LOADING . . . LOADING . . .

Digging the Tunnels

Now, the TBMs are started up. The spinning blades on the front of the TBM grind past the concrete wall of the launch pit. This is the beginning of drilling the long subway tunnels. The TBMs move slowly. The ground up dirt and rock is pulled through the TBM. Workers carry the dirt away in trucks.

- YEAR 1: People vote to build a new subway.
- YEAR 3: Civil engineers report where it will be safe to dig.
- YEAR 5: Architects and civil engineers give the city a complete plan.
- YEAR 6: The city orders TBMs and hires a contractor.
- YEAR 7: Construction workers begin digging big pits in the ground.
- YEAR 8: Workers put together the TBM parts.

The front of the TBM breaks through concrete at the end of the tunnel.

TBMs begin drilling the tunnels.

YEAR 9

. LOADING . . . LOADING . . .

The back end of the TBM builds the tunnel. **Mechanical** arms place segments to make concrete rings. The rings are sealed together to make the tunnels. Workers follow behind the TBMs. They string electric wires. They mount lights. They put together miles of subway tracks. After two years, the tunnels are complete.

The tunnel is made of segmented rings that fit tightly together.

- YEAR 1: People vote to build a new subway.
- YEAR 3: Civil engineers report where it will be safe to dig.
- YEAR 5: Architects and civil engineers give the city a complete plan.
- YEAR 6: The city orders TBMs and hires a contractor.
- YEAR 7: Construction workers begin digging big pits in the ground.
- YEAR 8: Workers put together the TBM parts.

TBMs begin drilling the tunnels.

YEAR 9

YEAR 11

LOADING . . . LOADING . . .

TBMs finish digging the tunnels.

Stations and Trains

Now it is time to work on the stations. Construction workers build all three at once. They make walls and floors inside the pits. Workers pour concrete and lay tiles. The places where people wait for the train are finished. Ticket booths are built. Finally, workers build stairs and elevators that go underground to the train.

YEAR 1: People vote to build a new subway.

YEAR 3: Civil engineers report where it will be safe to dig.

YEAR 5: Architects and civil engineers give the city a complete plan.

YEAR 6: The city orders TBMs and hires a contractor.

YEAR 7: Construction workers begin digging big pits in the ground.

YEAR 8: Workers put together the TBM parts.

The underground subway stops begin to take shape.

TBMs begin drilling the tunnels.

Workers begin building stations.

YEAR 9

YEAR 11

. . . LOADING . . .

TBMs finish digging the tunnels.

- YEAR 1: People vote to build a new subway.
- YEAR 3: Civil engineers report where it will be safe to dig.
- YEAR 5: Architects and civil engineers give the city a complete plan.
- YEAR 6: The city orders TBMs and hires a contractor.
- YEAR 7: Construction workers begin digging big pits in the ground.
- YEAR 8: Workers put together the TBM parts.

While the tunnels and stations are being built, train cars are being made. Factories make different parts of the train cars. The city then builds a place to put the parts together. The trains are assembled and moved to the tunnel. This building will be used for maintenance on the trains once they start running.

Train cars are put together in the maintenance building.

YEAR 9: TBMs begin drilling the tunnels.

YEAR 11: TBMs finish digging the tunnels.

Workers begin building stations.

YEAR 12: Subway train cars and maintenance building are finished.

OADING . . .

At last, the subway is done! The tunnels and stations are completed. The trains are assembled and on the tracks. But they are not yet ready for people to use. Do the stations' ticket booths work? Do the signals work? Workers test the train cars on the tracks. Engineers check for leaks in the tunnel. Everything is inspected and tested.

The inside of a subway car is ready for the first riders.

- YEAR 1: People vote to build a new subway.
- YEAR 3: Civil engineers report where it will be safe to dig.
- YEAR 5: Architects and civil engineers give the city a complete plan.
- YEAR 6: The city orders TBMs and hires a contractor.
- YEAR 7: Construction workers begin digging big pits in the ground.
- YEAR 8: Workers put together the TBM parts.

TBMs begin drilling the tunnels.

YEAR 9

Workers begin building stations.

YEAR 11

TBMs finish digging the tunnels.

YEAR 12

Subway train cars and maintenance building are finished.

The tunnels, stations, and trains are checked for safety.

YEAR 14

NG . . .

YEAR 1	YEAR 3	YEAR 5	YEAR 6	YEAR 7	YEAR 8
People vote to build a new subway.	Civil engineers report where it will be safe to dig.	Architects and civil engineers give the city a complete plan.	The city orders TBMs and hires a contractor.	Construction workers begin digging big pits in the ground.	Workers put together the TBM parts.

Opening Day

Today is the day! The city opens the new subway stations. Now people stream down into the stations. They buy their tickets. They step on the subway trains. They sit in their seats. Every day, people ride trains between the three stations. Traffic is better. It is time for the city to build the next section of subway!

A blue awning marks the stairs for a new subway station.

- YEAR 9: TBMs begin drilling the tunnels.
- YEAR 11: TBMs finish digging the tunnels.
- YEAR 11 → YEAR 12: Workers begin building stations.
- YEAR 12: Subway train cars and maintenance building are finished.
- YEAR 14: The tunnels, stations, and trains are checked for safety.
- YEAR 15: The subway opens for city travel.

GLOSSARY

architect Someone trained to design buildings and other structures.

civil engineer Someone trained to study a place and make plans for structures and buildings.

contractor A company that manages a building project; it hires workers, finds building materials, and makes sure the project is done on time.

detour A long way taken to avoid something.

earthquake fault A place where two sections of Earth move against each other and cause shaking.

excavator A big construction vehicle used for digging.

launch pit A hole in the ground where the tunnel boring machine will begin digging a new tunnel.

mechanical Having moving parts or machines to do a job.

station The place where people buy tickets and wait for trains; trains stop at stations to let people get on and off.

tunnel boring machine (TBM) A huge, round machine used for digging tunnels through soil and rock.

READ MORE

Kenney, Karen Latchana. *Building a Tunnel.* Mankato, Minn: Amicus Publishing, 2019.

Lassieur, Allison. *Subways in Action.* Mankato, Minn: Capstone Press, 2012.

McCarthy, Cecilia Pinto. *Engineering the NYC Subway System.* Minneapolis: ABDO Publishing, 2017.

WEBSITES

Crenshaw/LAX tunnel boring machine Harriet launch time-lapse
https://www.youtube.com/watch?v=5slUCkEyk0w

Time-lapse of digging of first Regional Connector tunnel
https://thesource.metro.net/2017/07/27/new-video-time-lapse-of-digging-of-first-regional-connector-tunnel/

Every effort has been made to ensure that these websites are appropriate for children. However, because of the nature of the Internet, it is impossible to guarantee that these sites will remain active indefinitely or that their contents will not be altered.

INDEX

ABOUT THE AUTHOR

Author Annie C. Holdren enjoys writing for children about engineering, technology, and the applications of science. She lives in California near a subway system that runs under the San Francisco Bay. Her favorite subway, though, is "The Tube" in London, England.